The Test Tutor

Verbal Comprehension Workbook

for the

WISC®-V Test

Test Tutor Publishing, LLC

Printed in the United States of America

TABLE OF CONTENTS

The Verbal Comprehension Subtests of WISC®-V Test Explained

The Wechsler Intelligence Scale for Children – Fifth Edition (WISC-V) is a widely used standardized test designed to assess the cognitive abilities of children aged 6 to 16. It provides a Full-Scale IQ score, representing general intellectual functioning, and five primary index scores: Verbal Comprehension, Visual-Spatial, Fluid Reasoning, Working Memory, and Processing Speed. Each index is derived from specific subtests that measure distinct cognitive skills. This workbook covers the Information, Vocabulary, Comprehension, and Similarities subtests, which fall under the Verbal Comprehension Index (VCI).

Information Subtest

What it Measures:
The Information subtest evaluates a child's general knowledge across various domains, such as science, history, geography, and culture. It reflects long-term memory, acquired knowledge, and the ability to retrieve and articulate factual information.

Administration:
The child is presented with a series of factual questions, which increase in difficulty as the test progresses. For example, questions might include "What is the capital of France?" or "What do fish use to breathe?"

Scoring:
Responses are scored as correct (1 point) or incorrect (0 points). Some questions allow partial credit for answers that are somewhat accurate but incomplete. The total score reflects the child's breadth of general knowledge and retrieval abilities.

Vocabulary Subtest

What it Measures:
This subtest assesses word knowledge and verbal concept formation. It is considered a strong indicator of overall verbal intelligence and educational experience.

Administration:
The child is asked to define words of increasing difficulty. For example, the examiner might ask, "What does 'happy' mean?" or "What is the meaning of 'philanthropy'?"

Scoring:
Responses are scored on a scale from 0 to 2 points based on accuracy, depth, and completeness. A precise definition earns 2 points, a partially correct answer earns 1 point, and an incorrect or unrelated answer earns 0 points.

Comprehension Subtest

What it Measures:
Comprehension evaluates practical reasoning, social judgment, and understanding of general principles. It measures the ability to apply learned concepts in real-world scenarios and interpret social norms or cultural practices.

Administration:
The child answers questions about common situations, social rules, or proverbs. For example, the examiner might ask, "Why should people wear seat belts?" or "What does 'the early bird catches the worm' mean?"

Scoring:
Responses are scored from 0 to 2 points based on relevance, insight, and appropriateness. Higher scores are given for answers that demonstrate deeper understanding or practical reasoning.

Similarities Subtest

What it Measures:
This subtest assesses abstract reasoning and verbal concept formation by requiring the child to identify similarities between paired items or concepts. It evaluates higher-order thinking, including categorization and the ability to identify relationships.
Administration:
The child is presented with pairs of words and asked how they are similar. For example, the examiner might say, "How are a dog and a cat alike?" or "How are freedom and responsibility alike?"

Scoring:
Responses are scored from 0 to 2 points. A score of 2 is awarded for abstract, conceptual answers (e.g., "Both are mammals"), while more concrete or superficial answers (e.g., "Both have four legs") receive 1 point. Incorrect or irrelevant answers score 0 points.

How to Use the Workbook

Each chapter of this book provides detailed descriptions of the subtests, scoring guidelines, and step-by-step instructions for administering the exercises. Carefully review each chapter, familiarize yourself with the exercises, and gather all necessary materials before beginning. You will need a stopwatch or clock for timing and a pencil to record your child's responses.

Explain to your child that you will be playing a series of fun games together and reassure them that they can take breaks whenever needed. During the session, if your child answers more than three consecutive questions incorrectly, consider allowing a short break or transitioning to a different activity. You can return to the unfinished subtest later to complete it.

To ensure optimal results, offer positive reinforcement and encourage your child to try their best independently. After completing the practice exercises, take the time to assess your child's strengths and areas for improvement.

Information

Description
During the information subtest your child will be asked to verbally respond to various questions about subjects in everyday life. Each correct response given within 30 seconds will receive 1 point.

Instructions
Ask the questions listed below. Try to elicit specific responses. If your child's answer is incomplete ask him "What do you mean?" or "Can you tell me more about that?" Begin by saying: **"Now, I'd like to ask you a few questions. Okay?"**

Question	Answers
1. Show me your hand.	(holds up hand)
2. Name something you drink.	Any consumable drink
3. Name a food.	Any food
4. How many fingers do you have?	10
5. What body part do you use to hear?	Ears
6. What day comes right after Friday?	Saturday
7. What month comes right after October?	November
8. How many legs does a dog have?	4
9. Name a kind of flower.	Daisy, Lily, Rose, Tulip, Violet, etc.
10. What kind of an animal is a sparrow?	Bird
11. Name a planet in outer space.	Mercury, Venus, Earth, Mars, Jupiter, Saturn, Uranus, Neptune
12. Name a musical instrument that people blow.	Saxophone, clarinet, flute, etc.
13. What happens to water when you heat it?	It boils
14. How many seasons are in a year?	4
15. How many minutes are in an hour?	60
16. What are gloves made of?	Fabric, cloth, material, leather, wool, cotton, etc.
17. In what season do the leaves fall?	Fall/Autumn
18. What do people use to talk to each other when they are in different locations?	Telephone, fax, email, letter, Internet, etc.
19. What body part digests food?	Stomach

Question	Answers
20. What body part circulates the blood?	Heart
21. What is an oak?	A type of tree
22. What is a fault line?	A place where two Teutonic plates meet, that when shifted cause earthquakes.
23. Name a famous landmark in Egypt.	Great Sphinx of Giza, Great Pyramid of Giza
24. How many people live in Asia?	Asia's population is about 4.4 billion - the greatest in the world.
25. What is the part of the Earth's atmosphere that blocks the sun's UV rays?	Ozone
26. Who is Leonardo da Vinci?	The artist that painted the Mona Lisa.
27. Tell me the directions of a compass.	North, South, East, West
28. Name a shape with 6 sides.	Hexagon
29. What measures atmospheric pressure?	Barometer
30. What measures air temperature?	Thermometer
31. What happens to a dinosaur bone when it stays in the ground for many years?	It becomes a fossil.
32. What is Newton's law of universal gravitation?	Isaac Newton developed the law that states that a particle attracts every other particle in the universe using a force that is directly proportional to the product of their masses and inversely proportional to the square of the distance between them.
33. What is Photosynthesis?	The process by which plants return oxygen to the air
34. What is Oxidation?	The chemical reaction between objects and oxygen that causes food to rot and metal to rust
35. What is Evolution?	The theory of natural selection developed by Charles Darwin
36. What is Chlorophyll?	The substance that makes leaves green
37. How many continents are in the world?	7
38. Name a famous Chinese philosopher.	Confucius, Laozi, Zou Yan, Mencius
39. How far is it from New York to London?	3,459 miles or 5,567 kilometers
40. Where is the Earth's highest point on dry land?	The summit of Mount Everest in Nepal.

Vocabulary

Description

The vocabulary subtest is administered in two parts: picture and verbal.

Picture Items **(for ages 6 to 7)**
Your child will be shown a picture and be asked to name it. He/she will be given 1 point for each correct answer.

Verbal Items **(for ages 6 to 16)**
Your child will be asked to define words that the examiner reads. Each answer receives 2, 1, or 0 points depending on its accuracy and specificity.

PICTURE ITEMS

Picture Item Instructions (pp. 10-28)

This subtest is administered only to children ages 6-7 years.
Because this subtest simply requires your child to identify objects, the best way to prepare is to make sure your child can identify as many objects as possible. The next exercise includes 114 pictures your child should review and be able to identify.

For each exercise, simply ask the question: **"What is this?"** If the answer is unclear, encourage your child to elaborate by asking "What do you mean?" or "Can you tell me more about it?" The answers are on page 29.

Verbal Item Instructions (pp. 32-34)

This subtest is administered to children ages 6-16 years.
Simply read the question and write down your child's response.

1

2

3

4

5

6

7

8

9

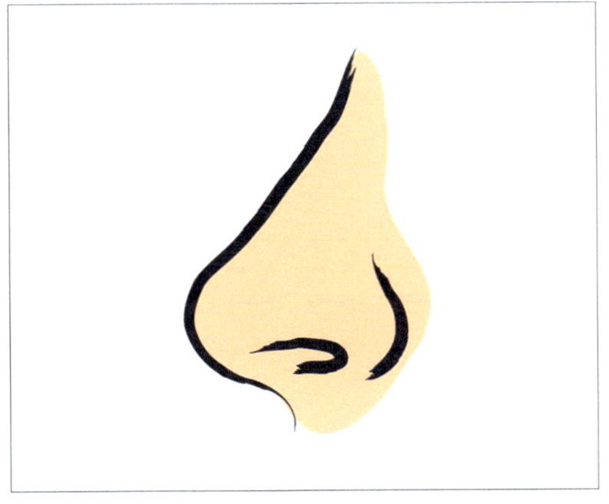

10

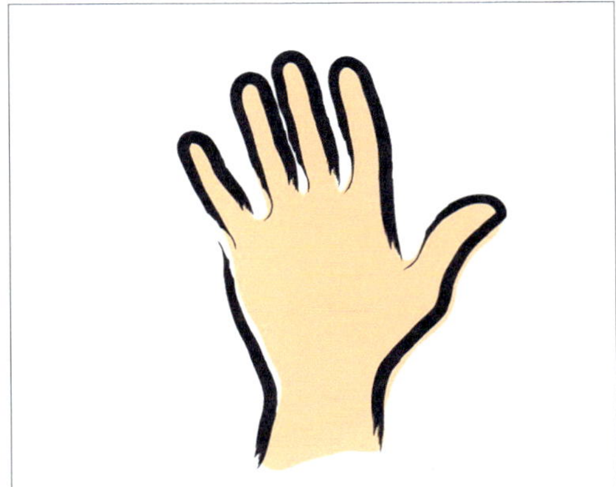

11

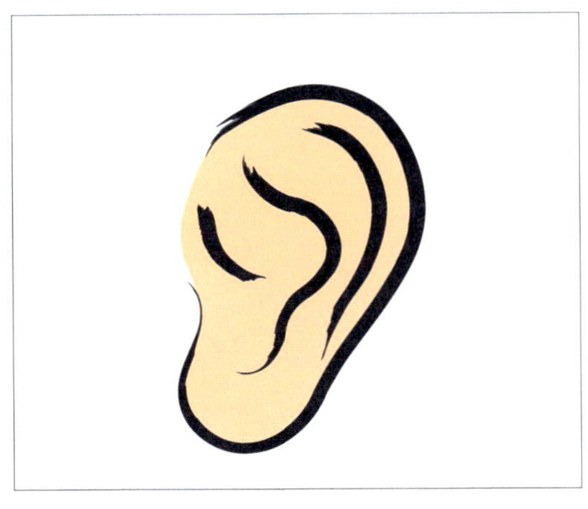

12

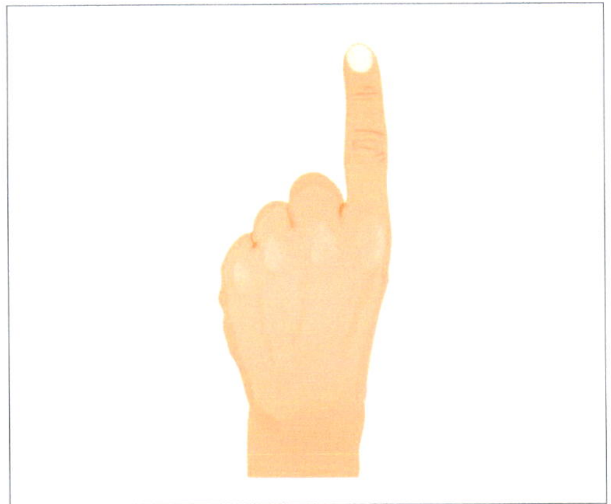

13

14

15

16

17

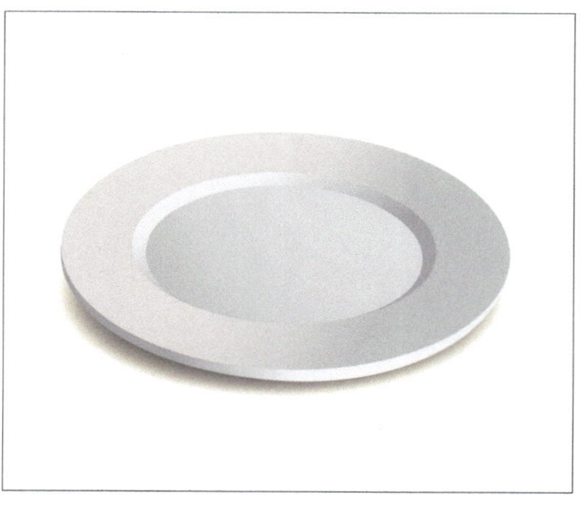

18

19

20

21

22

23

24

25

26

27

28

29

30

31

32

33

34

35

36

37

38

39

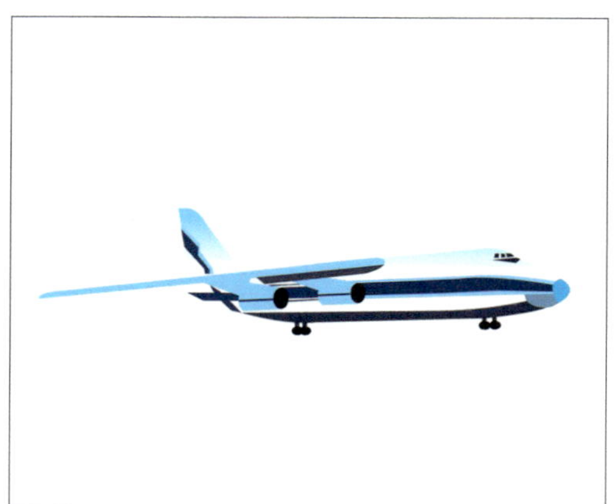

40

41

42

43

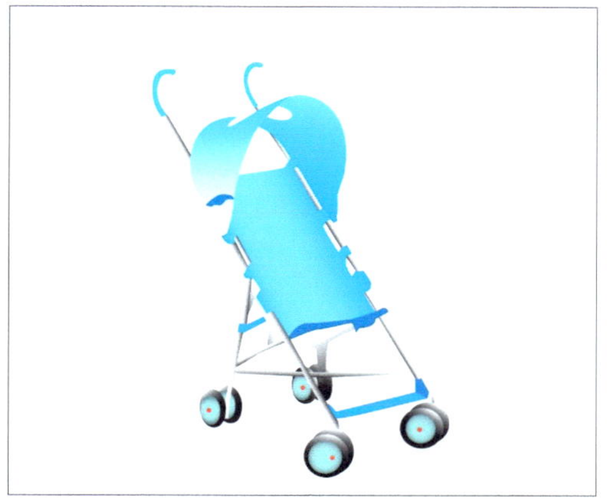

44

45

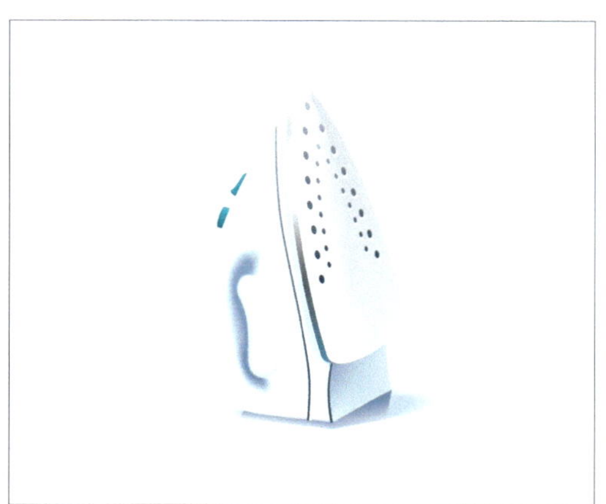

46

47

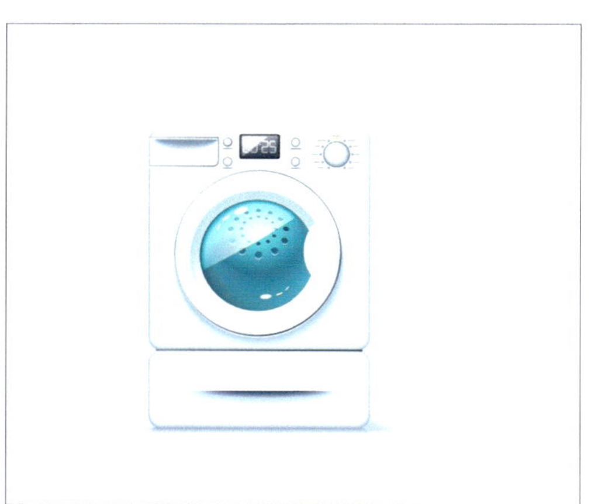

48

49

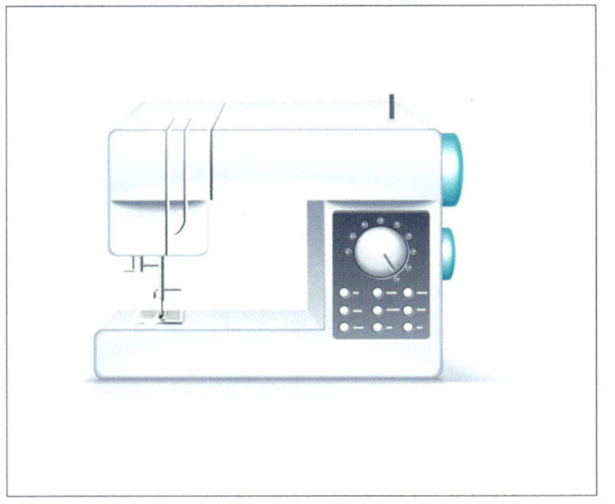

50

51

52

53

54

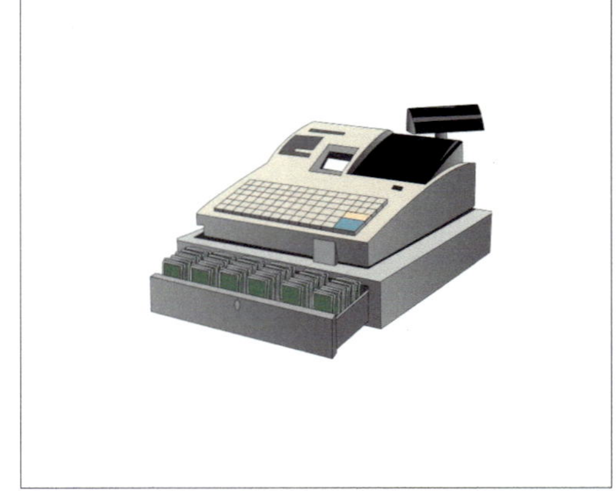

55

56

57

58

59

60

61

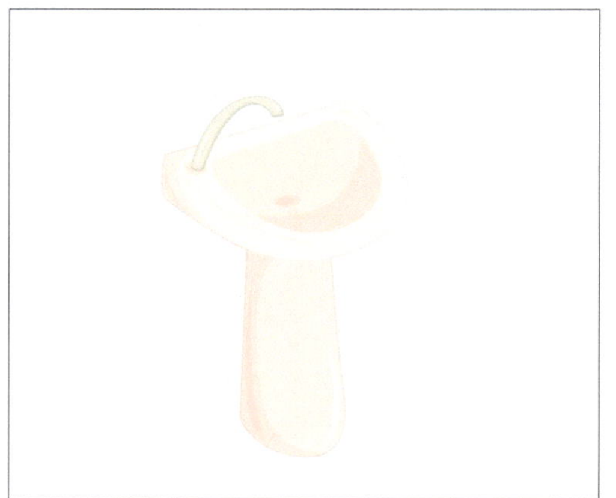

62

63

64

65

66

67

68

69

70

71

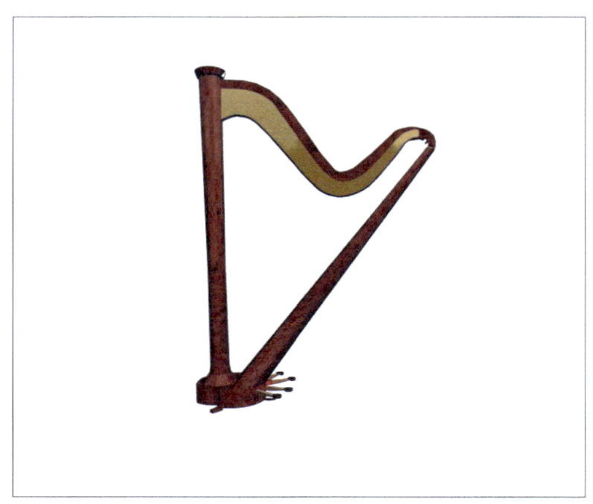

72

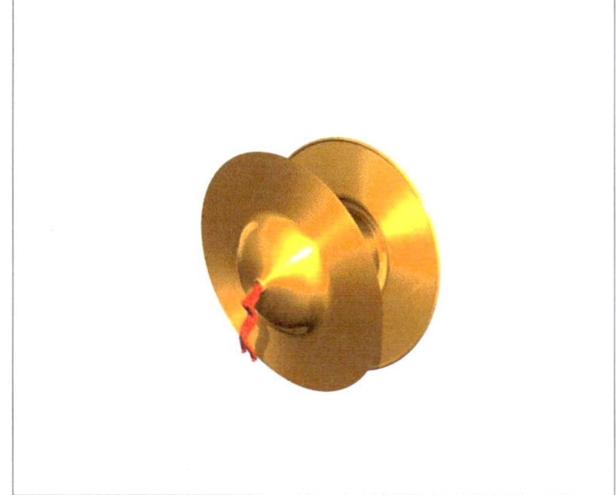

73

74

75

76

77

78

79

80

81

82

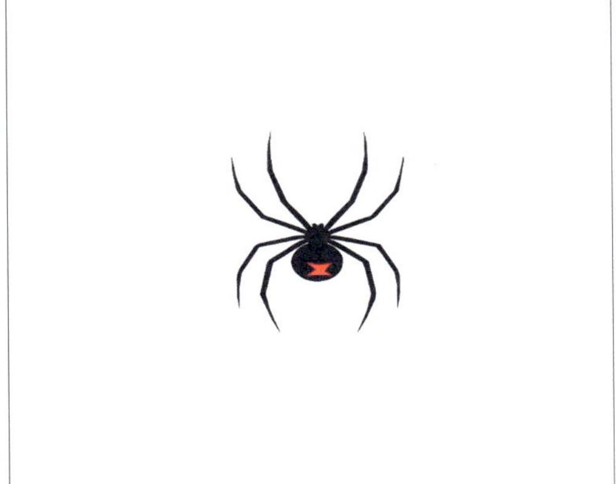

83

84

85

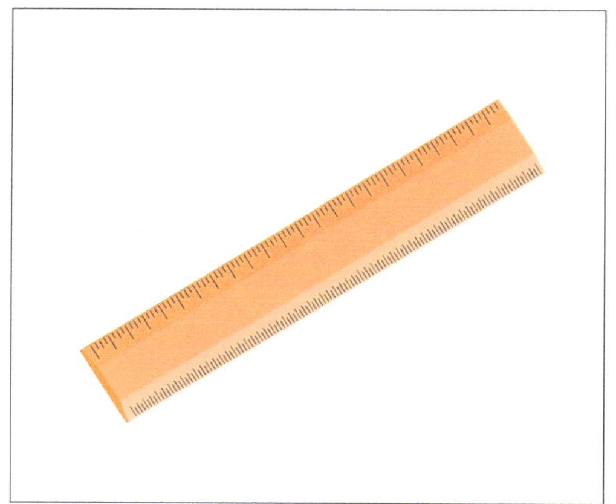

86

87

88

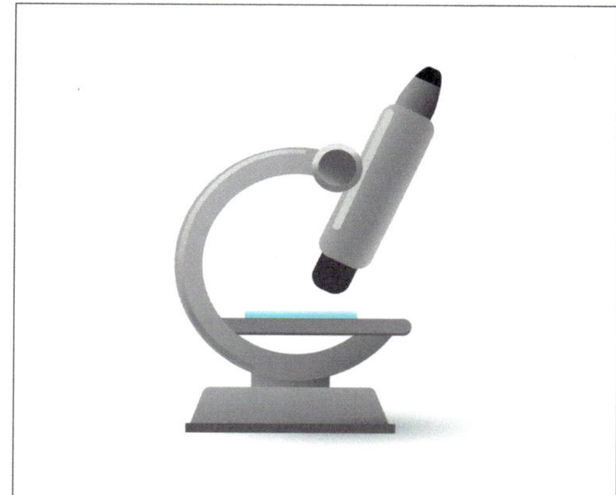

89

90

91

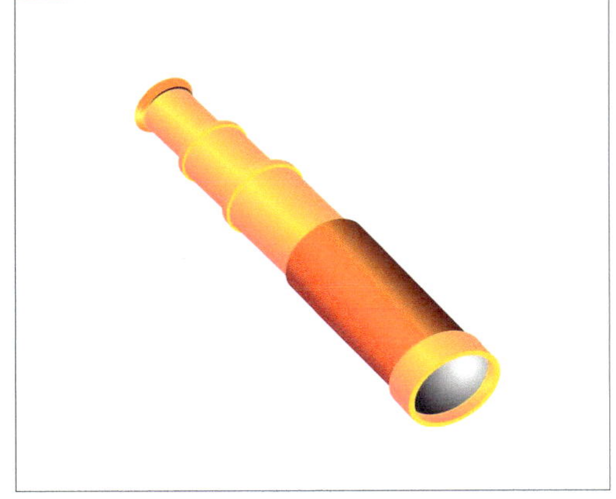

92

93

94

95

96

97

98

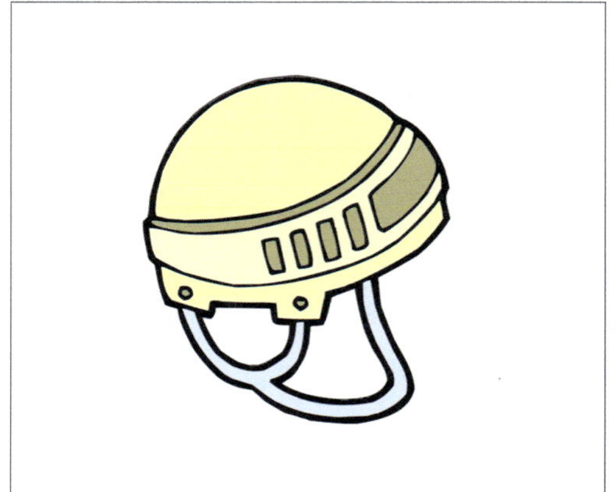

99

100

101

102

103
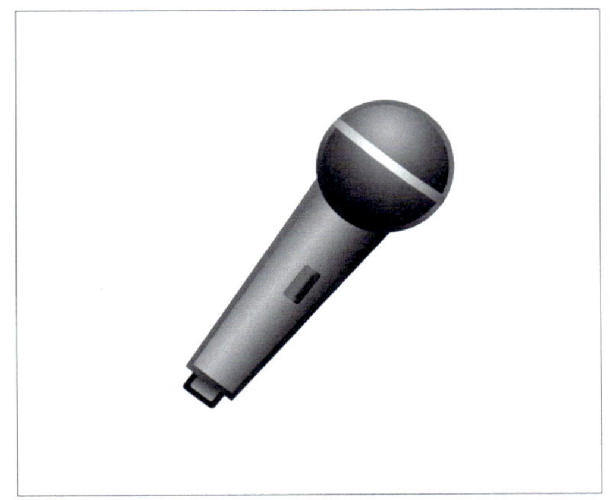

104

105

106
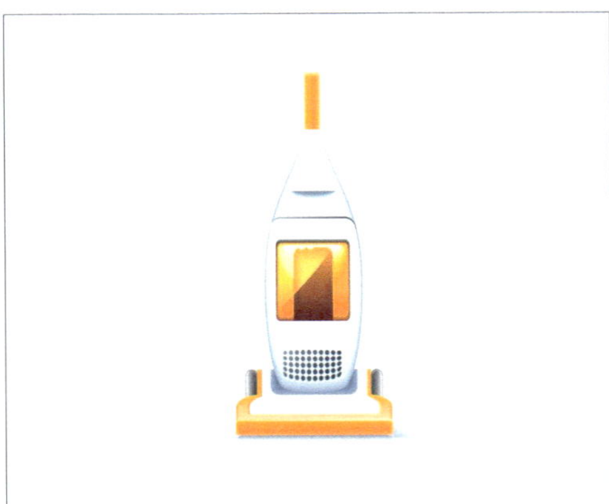

107

108
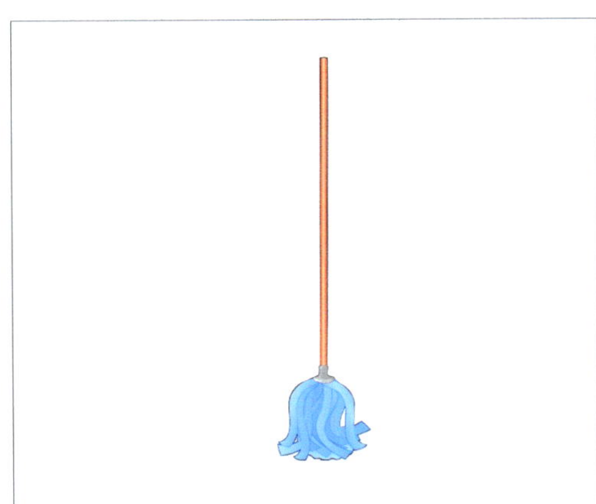

109

110

111

112

113

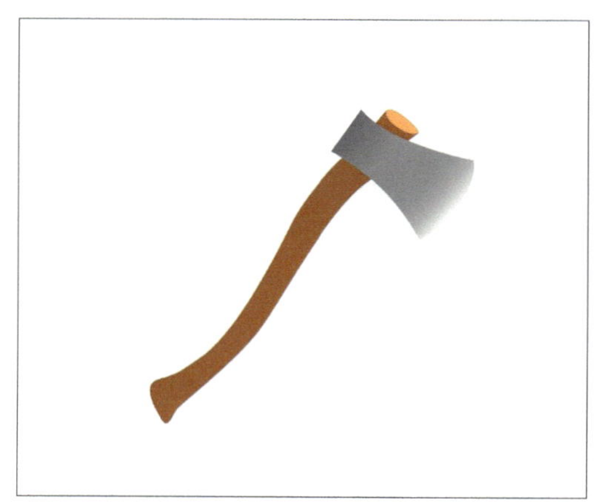

114

Picture	Answer
1	Cat
2	Dog
3	Cow
4	Duck
5	Turtle
6	Chicken
7	Mouth
8	Eye
9	Nose
10	Hand
11	Ear
12	Finger
13	Pot
14	Pan
15	Glass
16	Teapot
17	Plate
18	Cup
19	Strawberry
20	Apple
21	Banana
22	Grapes
23	Carrots
24	Pumpkin
25	Bread

Picture	Answer
26	Cheese
27	Chicken (meat)
28	Hamburger
29	Cupcake
30	Donut
31	Shirt
32	Shorts
33	Coat
34	Hat
35	Dress
36	Shoes/Sneakers
37	Car
38	Taxi
39	Airplane
40	Bus
41	Bicycle
42	Train
43	Stroller
44	Clock
45	Iron
46	Fan
47	Washing Machine
48	Stove
49	Sewing Machine
50	Hourglass

Picture	Answer
51	Lamp
52	Key
53	Shopping Cart
54	Cash Register
55	Television
56	Chair
57	Sofa/Couch
58	Bookcase
59	Bed
60	Table
61	Sink
62	Tub
63	Crane
64	Bulldozer
65	Tractor
66	Digger
67	Drum
68	Violin
69	Guitar
70	Piano
71	Harp
72	Cymbals
73	Flower
74	Tree
75	Tent

Picture	Answer
76	Igloo
77	Castle
78	House
79	Ladybug
80	Bee
81	Grasshopper
82	Spider
83	Snail
84	Butterfly
85	Ruler
86	Pencil
87	Globe
88	Microscope
89	Calculator
90	Scissors
91	Telescope
92	Crayon
93	Magnifying Glass
94	Football
95	Tennis Ball
96	Baseball
97	Hockey Stick & Puck
98	Helmet
99	Soccer Ball
100	Ice Skates

Picture	Answer
101	Basketball
102	Sled
103	Microphone
104	Newspaper
105	Sponge
106	Vacuum Cleaner
107	Broom
108	Mop
109	Lock
110	Hammer
111	Rake
112	Shovel
113	Axe
114	Nail

VERBAL ITEMS

Instructions

HINT: Your child should study these vocabulary words and look up their synonyms in a thesaurus.

Say: **"Now I'd like to play a word game. I'm going to ask you what some words mean. Let's start with Watch. What is a Watch?"**

1. What is a **Watch**? (something you wear that tells time)
2. What is a **Cap**? (a head covering; like a hat)
3. What is **Detergent**? (a cleanser, used for washing)
4. What is a **Dog**? (an animal that barks and has a tail)
5. What is a **Motorcycle**? (a vehicle with 2 wheels that you can ride)
6. What is a **Bathroom**? (a place where you take a bath/shower)
7. What is a **Glove**? (clothing to keep your hands warm)
8. What is a **Rat**? (an animal; rodent)
9. What is **Courage**? (bravery; fearlessness)
10. What is an **Award**? (something you get for winning a competition)
11. What is a **Burglar**? (a thief; a robber)
12. What is an **Aviator**? (a pilot of an airplane)
13. What does **Comply** mean? (to obey; to do as you are told)
14. What is a **Nuisance**? (an annoyance; a pest)
15. What is an **Isle**? (a small piece of land that is surrounded by water on all sides; like an island)
16. What does **Imitate** mean? (to copy; mimic)
17. What is a **Myth**? (a fable; a fairytale)
18. What does **Exact** mean? (precise; accurate)
19. What does **Translucent** mean? (clear; see through; transparent)
20. What does **Consumable** mean? (able to be eaten)
21. What is a **Law**? (a rule that is written to protect people from harm)
22. What does **Infrequent** mean? (rarely; seldom)

23. What does **Venerable** mean? (old and respected)
24. What is a **Consensus**? (when everyone agrees on something)
25. What does **Arduous** mean? (physically tough to do; strenuous)
26. What does **Nimble** mean? (moving quickly and lightly)
27. What does **Predict** mean? (to see into the future; foresight)
28. What does **Impending** mean? (about to occur at any moment; imminent)
29. What does **Nearsighted** mean? (able to see things that are close better than things that are faraway)
30. What is a **Modification**? (a change to fix something; a revision or amendment)
31. What does **Verbose** mean? (talking too much; garrulous; loquacious)
32. What does **Coerce** mean? (to force or compel someone to do something)
33. What does **Archaic** mean? (no longer in use; obsolete)
34. What does **Laggard** mean? (slow and pokey; dilatory)
35. What does **Specific** mean? (stated explicitly or precisely)
36. What does **Thrifty** mean? (economical; prudent; frugal)
37. What does **Balderdash** mean? (nonsense; foolishness)
38. What does **Repair** mean? (to fix something that was broken)
39. What is a **Champion**? (a person who saves people; a hero)
40. What is an **Audience**? (a group of people who watch or listen to something)
41. What does **Courteous** mean? (to be polite; to have manners)
42. What is an **Assistant**? (a person who helps)
43. What does **Calm** mean? (quiet and still)
44. What does **Patient** mean? (willing to wait)
45. What does **Amazement** mean? (great surprise)
46. What is **Midnight**? (12 o'clock at night)
47. Who are **Guests**? (people who are visiting in another house, restaurant, or hotel)
48. Who is a **Stranger**? (someone you don't know)

49. What does **Unusual** mean? (something that is different; not seen every day)
50. What is a **Vacation**? (a time to relax away from home)
51. What does **Overjoyed** mean? (really excited about something)
52. What is a **Transformation**? (a change in how something looks)
53. What is a **License**? (permission granted by the government to do something or own something)
54. What does **Enormous** mean? (very big)
55. What are **Diamonds**? (highly valued precious stones made from heated coal)
56. What is an **Invention**? (a new creation that makes our lives better)
57. What does **Amiable** mean? (friendly and approachable)
58. What is an **Anomaly**? (an abnormality; irregularity; aberration)

Comprehension

Description:
During the comprehension subtest, your child will be asked general questions about societal and social norms, rules, and consequences. Answers are given 2, 1, or 0 points based on accuracy and specificity.

Instructions:
Begin this subtest by telling your child that you are going to ask some questions and you want him/her to say the answer. Slowly ask the questions listed below. Repeat each question as necessary. If your child's answer is not clear, ask "What do you mean?" or "Can you tell me more about that?"

Question	Answers
1. Why do people wash their hands?	To keep them clean.
2. Why should people eat fruit?	Fruit keeps you healthy.
3. Why do cars have airbags?	To prevent injuries in a car accident.
4. What should you do if you see people stealing from a store?	Call the police.
5. What should you do if you see a small child wandering around by himself?	Ask an adult to look for the parents.
6. What should you do if your house catches fire?	Call 911.
7. What should you do if you find someone's keys on the school playground?	Turn them in to a teacher or administrator.
8. Why do people need watches?	To know the time; To make sure they are punctual.
9. Why should we recycle and save water?	To conserve energy, reduce pollution and save money.
10. Why do some teachers not allow students to bring toys to class?	Toys are a distraction and students need to pay attention in order to learn.
11. Why should children clean their rooms?	To learn independence and responsibility.
12. Why do drivers need to obey speed limits?	To avoid accidents.
13. What are the advantages of reading books versus watching TV?	Books give more detail and can be taken anywhere.
14. Why are elections important in a democracy?	So that everyone's voice is heard.
15. Why should you keep your word?	So that people will trust you.
16. Why do adults pay taxes?	To pay for schools, roads, etc.

Question	Answers
17. Why is it bad to "show off" when you win a game?	It may make other people feel bad about themselves.
18. Why do teachers need to be certified to teach?	To make sure they are qualified and keep current on new educational practices.
19. What are the advantages of having public schools?	All children have access to education whether that have money or not.
20. What does this saying mean? "Education is not the filling of a vessel but the lighting of a fire."	Learning is not about filling your mind with facts and data, but about igniting a student's interests and passions.
21. Why should people exercise regularly?	To stay healthy and strong.
22. Why is it good to admit fault when you make a mistake?	So that people know that you are sorry.
23. Why do students sometimes plant gardens, conduct science experiments, and go to museums?	Because experiences can teach information you can't learn in a classroom.
24. Why should you not play loud music late at night?	To be considerate of your neighbors.
25. Why do soldiers wear uniforms?	To demonstrate authority.
26. If someone picks a fight with you, what should you do?	Walk away; do not fight.
27. If you accidentally break something that belongs to someone else, what should you do?	Admit fault and apologize.
28. Why is it bad to lie?	People will not trust you.
29. What does this saying mean? "Don't spend time beating on a wall hoping to transform it into a door."	Don't continue to do the same thing repeatedly expecting a different result. Try a new approach to achieve your goals.
30. What should you do if you see that your neighbor has fallen and been badly hurt?	Call 911.
31. What does this saying mean? "A smooth sea never made a skillful mariner."	Stress can help motivate you to work harder, better and succeed.
32. Why is it bad for athletes to use drugs to enhance their performance?	It's unfair to the athletes who succeed through hard work.
33. What are some problems with the increased use of social media?	Poor face-to-face social skills, spread of false information, cyberbullying, lower grades
34. What does this saying mean? "As you sow, so shall you reap."	If you do good things, good things will happen to you. If you do bad things, bad things will happen to you.

Description
During the similarities subtest, the examiner asks the child to explain how two similar objects or concepts are similar.

Instructions
Read the sentences to your child. If the answer is not clear, ask "What do you mean?" or "Can you tell me more about that?" Begin by saying: **"Now I'm going to ask you a few questions about how things are alike. Let's start with..."**

1. How are a crayon and pencil alike? (things you write with)
2. How are orange juice and soda alike? (liquids; drinks)
3. How are a peach and a pear alike? (fruit)
4. How are a coat and a boot alike? (clothing)
5. How are a fly and a ladybug alike? (bugs; insects)
6. How are a pig and a goat alike? (animals)
7. How are pennies and nickels alike? (coins; money)
8. How are father and daughter alike? (family)
9. How are fall and spring alike? (seasons)
10. How are fear and sadness alike? (emotions)
11. How are a car and a plane alike? (vehicles; thing to travel in)
12. How are magazines and newspapers alike? (reading materials)
13. How are a restaurant and a grocery store alike? (places you can get food)
14. How are a house and an apartment alike? (places people live)
15. How are ice cream and snow alike? (cold)
16. How are bricks and cement alike? (building materials; used to make things)
17. How are cold and hot alike? (temperatures)
18. How are a scale and a ruler alike? (tools for measurement)
19. How are G and K alike? (letters)
20. How are 9 and 5 alike? (numbers)
21. How are blue and yellow alike? (colors)
22. How are breakfast and dinner alike? (meals)
23. How are tennis and baseball alike? (sports)
24. How are eyes and mouth alike? (parts of the face/5 senses)
25. How are rain and wind alike? (weather)
26. How are glue and nails alike? (they hold things together)
27. How are vapor and hail alike? (phases of water)
28. How are sweet and bitter alike? (tastes)
29. How are a bed and a sofa alike? (furniture)
30. How are a rose and a tulip alike? (flowers)

31. How are taste and touch alike? (senses)
32. How are morning and evening alike? (times of day)
33. How are pots and pans alike? (used for cooking)
34. How are cookies and cake alike? (sweets)
35. How are a lake and a volcano alike? (geographical elements)
36. How are a bedroom and kitchen alike? (rooms in a house)
37. How are pretty and ugly alike? (descriptions of appearance)
38. How are command and implore alike? (ways to get someone to do something or help you)
39. How are a finger and an elbow alike? (joints)
40. How are a grin and a frown alike? (facial expressions)
41. How are heat and electricity alike? (types of kinetic energy)
42. How are preparation and planning alike? (things that influence success)
43. How are a photographer and a writer alike? (artists)
44. How are beginning and end alike? (part of a sequence)
45. How are a hurricane and earthquake alike? (forces of nature)
46. How are a reflection and a footprint alike? (reproductions; duplications)
47. How are oxygen and water alike? (people need them to live)
48. How are retaliation and mercy alike? (choices you can make if someone hurts you)
49. How are consent and restriction alike? (ways to control)
50. How are alert and drowsy alike? (states of mind)
51. How are Confucius and Socrates alike? (famous philosophers)

Made in the USA
Columbia, SC
11 April 2025

56479305R00022